Chile

Chile emerged as an independent nation in 1810, after three centuries of Spanish rule. The country is very long and narrow — more than 4,500 kilometers (2,500 miles) from north to south and an average of 177 kilometers (110 miles) from the Andes Mountains in the east to the Pacific Ocean in the west.

Chile contains great contrasts of climate, culture and economy. In the north is the Atacama Desert, the driest place on earth. The area is sparsely inhabited, apart from a few Indian villages established long before the arrival of the Spaniards. The mining of copper and nitrates in the desert is declining, but copper is still important to the Chilean economy. The Mediterranean type of climate in central Chile is ideal for farming, and the capital, Santiago, is situated in this region. In southern Chile, cattle and sheep graze on land that has been cleared of forest, but in the bleak and barren country of the far south, there are few settlers and communication is difficult.

Alex Huber is a Chilean photo-journalist who has traveled extensively throughout his native country, and as far afield as Antarctica, to gather these twenty-six accounts of life in Chile.

PERU

BOLIVIA

BRAZIL

PARAGUAY

Chungara Lake

Arica

Iquique
Pica

DESERT

Maria Elena
Calama

ATACAMA

Antofagasta

PACIFIC OCEAN

ARGENTINA

Coquimbo • La Serena

URUGUAY

Mt Aconcagua

Valparaiso
Santiago

Rancagua

Curico
Talca

Concepción • Chillán

Los Angeles

Osorno
Puyehue

Puerto Montt

CHILOÉ ISLAND

Coihaique

Punta Arenas • Cerro Sombrero

TIERRA DEL FUEGO

MAGELLAN STRAITS

CAPE HORN

we live in
CHILE

Alex Huber

The Bookwright Press
New York · 1986

Living Here

We live in Argentina
We live in Australia
We live in Brazil
We live in Britain
We live in Canada
We live in the Caribbean
We live in Chile
We live in China
We live in Denmark
We live in East Germany
We live in France
We live in Greece
We live in Hong Kong
We live in India
We live in Indonesia
We live in Ireland
We live in Israel

We live in Italy
We live in Japan
We live in Kenya
We live in Malaysia and Singapore
We live in Mexico
We live in the Netherlands
We live in New Zealand
We live in Pakistan
We live in the Philippines
We live in Poland
We live in South Africa
We live in Spain
We live in Sweden
We live in the Asian U.S.S.R.
We live in the European U.S.S.R.
We live in West Germany

Further titles are in preparation

To Isabel for her constant support.

First published in the United States in 1986 by
The Bookwright Press
387 Park Avenue South
New York, NY 10016

First published in 1985 by
Wayland (Publishers) Ltd
61 Western Rd, Hove
East Sussex BN3 1JD, England

© Copyright 1985 Wayland (Publishers) Ltd

ISBN 0–531–18023–9
Library of Congress Catalog Card Number: 85–72744

Phototypeset by Kalligraphics Ltd
Redhill, Surrey
Printed in Italy by G. Canale & C.S.p.A., Turin

Contents

"The wind drives me crazy"

Sergio Santelices, 39, is married and has three children. He was born in Santiago, and came to Punta Arenas when he was a child. He owns a ranch outside Punta Arenas, with 5,500 sheep and 630 head of cattle.

This part of Chile is called Magallanes, after the Magallanes (Magellan) Strait which was discovered by a Spanish sailor called Hernando de Magallanes (Ferdinand Magellan). His ship was the first to circumnavigate the world.

Herding cattle on the estancia *near Punta Arenas.*

Punta Arenas was founded in 1848, by a Chilean army officer. The first Europeans arrived twenty years later. They decided to try stock farming, and the first three hundred sheep were brought from the Falkland Islands. The area had previously been inhabited only by nomadic

Indians, who lived by fishing and hunting guanacos, animals related to the llama.

By the beginning of this century, the wool industry was well developed. Huge *estancias* (ranches) were established and leased by the State to private farmers. These have since been divided into smaller *estancias*, which are much easier to maintain.

I came to own my *estancia* after the last big distribution of land, in 1978. *Estancias* of 5,000 hectares (12,355 acres), with 5,000 sheep, were offered for sale. Applicants were required to be from the region and to have cattle-ranching experience. I was able to meet these requirements, and so bought my farm.

In Magallanes, it is commonly accepted that 5,000 is a sufficient number of animals to provide a farmer with a living. The sale of the meat pays for the running of the farm, and the wool pays for living expenses.

The climate in this part of the world is very harsh. Winters are cold and summers are very windy. I prefer the winter, when the cold is easier to cope with — the constant sound of wind in summer drives me crazy! But although the climate is harsh for humans, it isn't for sheep. Good quality grass which is resistant to cold and wind allows our animals to produce very high quality wool. Our main buyers come from England, France and Italy.

Traditionally, we have always bred sheep in Magallanes, but during the sixties, people started breeding cattle. I have 630 head of cattle, which I sell at Santiago. The 3,000 kilometer (1,800 mile) journey by truck through Argentina takes between seven and ten days. But a transport ship now operates from Punta Arenas to Puerto Montt, taking only two days. From there to Santiago, the journey is only 1,000 kilo-meters (621 miles) on good roads.

The sheep-shearing season is from December to February, when farmers contract shearers to do the work. They are skilled and do their job very fast. A good shearer takes two minutes to shear a sheep. Groups of twenty-six men will shear 1,200 to 1,300 animals in a day. At my *estancia*, the work takes five or six days. The rest of the year I work the estancia with only two workers. The wool is usually sold unwashed in bales to independent buyers who travel around the region buying wool.

Soon we will have to move to the city so that our children can go to secondary school. Although I love living in the country, I suppose that I will soon get used to traveling to my *estancia* from Punta Arenas, two or three times a week.

Sergio with his sons, on his estancia.

"I look after flamingos and vicuñas"

Hernán Rojas, 25, is unmarried and has been a game warden at the Lauca National Park, in the Andes, for three years. This is one of sixty-six national parks in Chile, and is located on the Chilean Plateau, which stretches to the border with Bolivia.

This national park, high in the Andes, was created in 1970. Within the park are the Chungará Lake and the Painacota Volcano, which both attract many visitors. Chungará is the highest lake in the world — 4,300 meters (13,420 feet) above sea level. It is quite a small lake, but it has an interesting legend connected with it.

According to legend, the place used to be a rich, fertile valley with plenty of water and grass for the animals. It was inhabited by pagan people. One day, during one of their special feasts, the Sun God came down to them, dressed as a beggar. He asked for water but nobody would give it to him except a young woman with her baby. In gratitude, he told her that she must leave the valley at once because a great disaster was about to occur. He told her not to look back, no matter what she heard. The woman immediately left the valley with her baby, but when she arrived at the foot of the Painacota Volcano, she heard a great noise behind her and could not resist looking back. She was immediately turned to stone. To this day, on the far side of the lake, there is a strange rock that looks like a woman with a baby on her back.

Nowadays the Chungará Lake is of great importance, because from here water is pumped to the port of Arica, 210 kilometers (130 miles) away, across the Atacama Desert.

At this altitude many tourists suffer from *la puna*, a condition causing headaches and sleepiness due to lack of oxygen. When this happens, the best remedy is to drink *chachacome*, an infusion made from a herb used by the local Indians when they are unwell.

The people who live here are Aymara Indians. They came originally from Bolivia and Peru, when the Inca Empire expanded during the fourteenth century. They are farmers and shepherds, herding flocks of llamas, guanacos and sheep.

I live in a game warden's hut which has three bedrooms, a kitchen and bathroom. Tourists sometimes stay here, to study the

Painacota Volcano and Chungará Lake, in the Lauca National Park.

birds, plants and animals and to fish in the rivers. I protect the birds and animals in the park, although I do not carry a gun. Among the creatures I look after are flamingos and vicuñas. The vicuña is a delicate, shy animal, related to the camel family, and it grazes freely in the park. It is found only in South America and is highly prized for its wool, which is ideal for warm woolen clothing, essential in our cold winters. Vicuña wool fetches a high price at market.

Temperatures up here can reach minus 20°C (−4°F) and the lake usually freezes over in winter. People in this area used to burn a resinous plant called *yareta* to warm themselves on cold nights. When it is burned the plant gives off an extraordinary amount of heat, similar to coal. It grows only 1 cm (½ inch) a year and lives for more than a hundred years. But it was used so extensively for fuel that it became nearly extinct. Now the plant is protected, and with the arrival of liquid gas and kerosene, the plant's survival is no longer in danger.

Wild llamas graze peacefully in the beautiful National Park.

"Skydiving is a way of life"

Isabel Margarita Soto, 28, is a freelance computer engineer living in Santiago. Four years ago she began skydiving, and is the only woman in the record-holding Chilean Parachute Formation team.

The first "free jump" is the occasion when skydivers really feel they are flying. The first five trial jumps are made with a cord that automatically opens the parachute. When pupils have proved to their instructor that they are able to open the parachute themselves, they are ready for what is called the first free jump.

After the first free jump, skydivers may be initiated by other members of the club, by having their heads shaved and rubbed with oil and paint. Then they may be thrown into the club swimming pool!

In the plane, just before the jump.

"When I am flying through the air . . . I forget all about fear."

usual.

Every skydiver jumps with two parachutes; the main and the reserve. The reserve is packed by a "rigger" who specializes in packing reserve parachutes. These should be opened and repacked every three months, although some of us forget to do this and only open them once a year. This can be dangerous – if it doesn't open when it is needed . . . !

I skydive every weekend at our center at Chinihue, near Santiago, making two or three jumps a day. The cost of jumps depends on the height from which we dive. We go up in a Cessna airplane and jump from a height of 2,743 meters (9,000 feet). From this height we have almost one minute of diving, and during this time we execute different formation figures such as "stars," "diamonds" and so on. The more difficult the figure the more we enjoy performing it.

In a way, skydivers have realized the eternal human dream of flying. One minute of "flying" in the sky is quite different from one minute on earth. Up there time goes slowly and we can plan our movements without hurry.

There are about 300 skydivers in Chile. Most of us are from Santiago – there are eight clubs in the city. I dive with the Scorpions Club, which is the largest.

Recently, Chile beat the Brazilian-held South American Parachute Formation record. I was the only woman on the team and the only woman ever to be on a South American record-breaking team. Now we are training to beat our own record, with a formation of 22 skydivers. For the second year in a row, I have been Women's National Parachute Champion.

For me and all real skydivers, skydiving is a way of life. Emotionally I feel I really need to "fly" every week.

At first, every parachute jump is made with feelings of fear. I'm sure everybody feels a moment of tension during the plane flight, before reaching the right altitude for the jump. I certainly do, but the moment I leave the plane the tension disappears. When I feel myself flying through the air and I'm aware that I can move my body up or down, forward or backward, I forget all about fear. But many people never overcome their fears, especially if they have experienced a parachute's not opening properly. Some skydivers have never had a parachute failure: I've had five failures in 500 jumps, which is quite

"Rodeos are our national sport"

Hugo Navarro is 25. He was born in San Bernardo, a small village near Santiago. He was only 5 when his father first gave him a horse. He works at a stud farm, breeding and training horses for rodeos.

I work on a farm near Curico, a city with a population of 150,000 situated in what is called the "Zone Huasa" of Chile. This is part of the Chilean Central Valley, which extends from Santiago in the north, down to Chillán in the south.

Rodeos, which are the national sport of Chile, are frequently held in the region. I have been involved with the sport all my life. Like my father and grandfather, I train horses for the rodeos.

The Spaniards originally brought horses to South America. In Chile, the horses evolved according to the geographical characteristics of the country. A typical Chilean horse is not too tall, and is very strong. Our horses are intelligent, obedient, manageable and docile, and these characteristics make them ideal for rodeos. This is a fast and dangerous sport, very demanding for both riders and horses.

Rodeos started during the nineteenth century in Santiago, when people went into the surrounding countryside once a year to collect the cattle for marking and selling. It became a festival, where animals were brought to the main square and riders showed off their skills in leading cattle. In time, this practice grew into a sport,

Hugo uses a specially-trained cow so that his horses can practice for the rodeo.

with definite rules that haven't changed for more than 150 years.

Rodeos take place inside a *media luna* (half moon), which is a circular track surrounded by a timber fence. The mounted competitors take part in pairs and they ride into the middle of the circle. When it is their turn, they enter a smaller half circle to wait for a young bull, which has never been in a *media luna* before. When the animal enters, the two riders guide it twice around the ring. Then a gate is opened and the bull starts running around the *media luna* with one rider behind, pushing, and the other rider beside it. This is a very difficult maneuver for horse and rider because the horse's flank must not touch the bull. The run is 66 meters (216 feet) to a mark, where the rider who has been beside the bull tries to stop it, by pressing the animal against the timber fence with the chest of his horse. Depend-

ing on where the horse touches the bull, the pair receive points; ranging from zero when it is touched by the horse on the head or neck, to 4 when the bull is stopped at his back legs – the most difficult place for the horse. Later the riders change places and run in the opposite direction, repeating the performance.

Rodeos take place all over Chile and the great hope of everyone involved in the sport is to take part in the National Championship at Rancagua, held every year in March. Last year I won the Championship with a friend, and it was the most fantastic experience of my life.

Rodeo is a completely amateur sport. It is a tradition that the pair who win the rodeo dance the *cueca* – national dance – with the queen of the rodeo.

Finalists at the 1984 Championship in Rancagua.

"We try to maintain our own traditions"

Justino Colemar is an Aymara Indian. He is 68 years old and lives with his two sons in a village in the Caspana Valley, in the Chilean Altiplano, 80 kilometers (50 miles) from the nearest town, Calama.

My family has lived in the Caspana Valley for generations. Long before the Spaniards arrived, the village was under the domination of the Incan Empire.

Nowadays we all feel Chilean. We live

An Aymara Indian woman drives cattle and sheep to graze.

under the law of Chile, and since 1978 we have been integrated educationally with the rest of the country because we now have a big elementary boarding school. The school takes students from here and from all the surrounding villages as well. The education at the school is especially aimed at improving methods of agricul-

ture, which is our main activity in the Caspana Valley.

The Caspana Valley is nearly 3,000 meters (1,000 feet) high in the Altiplano. But in spite of its height, the valley is so enclosed that the climate is suitable for growing fruit and vegetables.

We have no television because TV channels cannot reach here. Although we are subjected to strong cultural influences from outside, we try to maintain our own traditions, especially regarding our religious festivals. Religion for us is a mixture of the Catholic faith and our own ancestral beliefs, in which the earth and the sun play an important role. During the first three days of February we celebrate our village festival, in honor of the Virgin of Guadalupe, patron saint of the village. Our church, located in the old part of Caspana, on the cliffs overlooking the valley, is one of the oldest in Chile.

Eighty families live in Caspana — 500 people altogether. Almost everybody has a piece of land on which they grow vegetables such as onions and lettuce, as well as apple, apricot and fig trees. The women of the village sell our produce in Calama. They travel to the town by car or bus. It was not until 1930 that we got a road to Caspana. Before that the village was totally isolated and people had to walk all the way to Calama, which was very tiring. Because of this isolation, there was much intermarriage in the village and everybody here is related.

Now, with the recently improved road, tourists come here and many villagers sell souvenirs to them.

In the old days we used to have more grass because there was more rain, and we were able to keep animals in the village. Nowadays we have very little rain and we can only keep about 1,000 animals —

Carefully cultivated plots of land in front of a typical Aymara house.

llamas, guanacos, goats and sheep, which are looked after by the women and children.

We have a system of community work in the village where people work together on a project that benefits everybody. For instance, a few years ago, all the people of the village worked to restore the roof of our church.

At present I am helping one of my sons to build a house where he will live with his wife and child. My father did this for me when I was young. My other son is also helping to build the house, and we have been working on it for fifteen days. It will take the three of us another twenty days to finish, working ten hours a day. We load trucks with earth and rocks which we bring from a stone quarry nearby. The rocks are volcanic and the big ones weigh about 15 kilograms (33 lb). We use straw to roof the houses.

"Food arrives only once a month"

Ana Maria Martino is married to a lieutenant in the Chilean Air Force, stationed at King George Island in Antarctica. She and her husband and five families belong to the first Chilean colonization plan for Antarctica.

We arrived in Antarctica in December 1983, for a two-year period. Soon another six families will join us. I am glad they are coming because their arrival will make our life here much more interesting. Among them will be a teacher so we will

The Antarctic base is a long way from civilization, as this signpost indicates.

have a proper elementary school for the children.

Last year the children were taught by the six women on the base, in turn — two of us teaching for a month at a time. The children learned reading, writing and arithmetic much earlier than they would have at school in Santiago. Of course, we have much more time here to spend with our children and families are very united.

There is little space at the base in which the children can play and they have to spend a lot of time inside the houses. But their presence is important in the life of the base, especially for those men who have left their families behind. The children here have many kind "uncles" who give them presents!

The houses on the base are very comfortable. Ours has three bedrooms, living room, playroom, kitchen and bathroom. All cooking and heating is by electricity.

Life in Antarctica is different from anywhere else. During winter, when only eighty people remain (there are 230 in summer), our house becomes almost covered with snow. The monthly supply plane is frequently unable to land and we may have to wait a couple of months for new supplies.

We keep in touch with friends and relatives in Chile, more than 8,000 kilometers (5,000 miles) away by short wave radio. The short wave radio world is fascinating: it is full of kind amateurs who help us to speak with our people on the mainland.

It is challenging to be a housewife in Antarctica. Because food arrives only once a month, I have had to learn certain tricks to keep things fresh. I squeeze the juice of lemons and freeze it in cubes, and I freeze the peel to use in cakes. I also beat fresh eggs and freeze them into portions. I dry lettuce leaves thoroughly and store them in plastic bags in the refrigerator, where they keep for a month or more. I store other fruit and vegetables in the hallway between the outer and inner door of the house, where the temperature is just about at the freezing point.

Summers are our best season. The snow melts, exposing dark, arid soil, with lichen and moss. The temperature goes up to 10°C (50°F), which is high compared to our winters, when temperatures remain permanently below zero. The nights never get completely dark in summer, although in winter we have only four hours of daylight.

But none of us regret coming here. I know about Antarctic plants and animals and I've learned First Aid and skiing. I've also learned about the Antarctic Treaty, which dedicates Antarctica to peaceful objectives and forbids its use for military purposes. The signatories of the treaty, of which Chile is one, have established research stations on Antarctica. We have Russians and Chinese as neighbors, and other bases on the island include survey teams from Poland, Argentina and Brazil.

A view of the base in summer time.

"The weather changes very fast"

Ernesto Hein owns an airline with planes operating in the remote 11th Region, in the south of Chile. He also owns the most southerly hot spring in Chile, in one of the wettest areas of the world.

When I was 8 years old, I saw two planes colliding over the bay at Puerto Montt. This accident made a great impression on me and I decided that I would learn all about planes when I grew up.

When I was 15, my uncle taught me to fly, and I was immediately captivated. I must now be one of the few pilots in the country with more than 22,000 hours' flying time – this is equal to flying around the earth 130 times!

As a pilot I have had many curious experiences. Once, I was forced to land on the main street of Coyhaique with a sick passenger. As this had never happened in the town before, the police didn't know what to do. The problem was solved with a ticket for illegal parking!

My airline now has two planes, each carrying eight passengers. We used to have more planes, operating in the southern region of Chile, where roads were few and villagers were more familiar with planes than they were with cars. Now, many roads have been built, but planes are still essential to reach the remote villages. But a pilot who flies in this region must be very experienced, as the weather changes quickly, and this is one of the wettest regions in the world.

One of the many natural hot spring pools at Puyuhuapi.

The most important road here is the 400-kilometer (248-mile) long Austral Road. It was finished in 1982, and in many parts is only single lane. It goes through deep forest, mountains and places where humans have never been before. The road has linked this region to the rest of the country and tourism has grown enormously. Now, the rest of Chile is beginning to know the region.

Coyhaique, the regional capital, was founded only fifty years ago. When settlers first began arriving in the 1930s, traveling through Argentina and across the Andes, huge fires were lit to clear the land for agriculture and cattle ranching. The fires sometimes burned for twelve months and the remains of burnt trees can be seen everywhere.

I own a hot spring at Puyuhuapi, which I bought from an old Chono Indian. Puyuhuapi means "where the *puyes* meet." *Puyes,* are very small fish. The Chono Indians were the first inhabitants of this place. They always came to the hot springs during the winter.

There are twenty-four springs at Puyuhuapi. The whole area is volcanic and the temperature of the spring water varies between 24°C and 85°C (75°F and 185°F). Puyuhuapi is a beautiful place, where nature can be experienced at its most magical. One of my favorite pastimes is to bathe in the main pool, where the water is 45°C (113°F), while outside it is raining and temperatures are just above freezing.

Now, with the Austral Road, it is easy to reach Puyuhuapi. Then, a thirty-minute boat trip brings us to the hot springs. Before the road was built, we had to fly from Coyhaique.

Yachtsmen come here from all over the world. Every season, between November and March, at least thirty yachts come to visit us. We have cottages to accommodate tourists and we are building more.

Low tide at Puyuhuapi hot springs.

"King crab is a gourmet delicacy"

Jorge Barcenas is 22, married and has a baby daughter. He was born in Puerto Montt and has been in Punta Arenas for the past ten years. He works for a big company which specializes in fishing for king crabs near Cape Horn.

My job is difficult because of the terrible weather conditions in the area where I work. I catch crabs in the Wollaston Islands, which are near Cape Horn, at the extreme south of the continent.

We work for nine months of the year.

Unloading king crabs to be taken to the factory for cleaning, tasting and canning.

The remaining three months are winter, when the weather is too severe to work. Then, the king crabs are left alone to breed. Their numbers are becoming smaller, so our catches are strictly regulated. We are only allowed to catch male crabs larger than 12 centimeters (5 inches). The females are left alone. We can tell a female crab because it is smaller than the male

and has a red mark on its belly.

King crabs are found in the sea off the southern coasts of Chile, at a depth of 30 meters (90 feet). We catch them using traps which we place on the sea bottom. We use the heads and tails of fish as bait. The traps are made of steel and net and are cone-shaped. They have a hole with a rubber seal at the top, and the bait is placed at the bottom. When the king crab crawls in through the hole, the rubber seal keeps it from getting out again.

Twenty traps are ranged in a line, called a "mother line." My boat, with a crew of five, is in charge of thirty "mother lines." We are therefore responsible for 600 traps.

We spend up to six months without returning to Punta Arenas. But we have contact with civilization because each week a transport vessel calls to collect all the king crabs from the eighteen boats belonging to our company. During the peak months, November and December, the company sends up to three transport boats each week, to collect our catch. The transport vessels are very important to us because they bring supplies and news from home. They also take us back to Punta Arenas, if necessary.

King crabs, with their long legs, move very slowly. They are very fragile and look quite prehistoric. The transport vessels must carry them alive in special tanks filled with clean oxygenated sea water. If a crab dies, after only two hours the flesh becomes sour and poisonous and impossible to eat.

When the crabs arrive at the factory, they are killed by separating the legs from the shell. The legs are washed and cooked for ten minutes in boiling sea water and the flesh is then removed. This is a delicate operation requiring patience, and is carried out by women. Then the crabmeat

The delicious king crab meat in plastic-covered cans, ready to be sealed.

is tested for quality – the best pieces come from the section of the leg nearest the shell. After that the meat is ready to be frozen or canned.

Our crabs are mainly for the international market. We sell to Europe and to the United States. King crabs are very expensive and I believe that in the U.S. a portion can cost up to $30. King crab is a gourmet delicacy; the meat is white and red, very tender and with a strong taste. It is usually eaten with lemon or a sauce, and it is delicious.

"I have won more than a hundred medals"

Felipe Ojeda, age 10, goes to an English school in Santiago. He also does BMX (bicycle motorcross) racing, which he and his family take very seriously. During 1982, he became World Champion in the 8-year-old junior category, in Ohio in the United States.

In our country, education is divided into elementary, which lasts eight years, and secondary, which lasts four years. Students can then go on to a university or continue to study at one of Chile's many technical colleges.

All Chilean children have to attend elementary school, and many go to state-owned free schools, which ensure that they all complete a period of elementary education. At these schools, pupils get a free glass of milk and special crackers, full of vitamins and proteins. Secondary education at state schools is almost free, too. Pupils have only to pay a small entrance fee. This system of education has made illiteracy almost unknown in Chile.

I am in the sixth grade at my school and I study seven subjects; math, Spanish, English, art, science, writing and sports. My favorite subjects are math and Spanish. I would like to become an engineer, but I suppose there is plenty of time to think about that in the future.

At the moment, my main concern is BMX racing. I practice all week in the neighborhood near my home, and on Tuesdays and Fridays on the race track, if we are going to race on the following Sunday. I have the wholehearted support of my family in my sport. For kids of my age, it would be difficult to practice BMX seriously if the family were not involved. My dad trains me and my mother takes me to the race track during the week. She also takes me to karate classes three times a week – I have a green belt in karate.

BMX racing is like a game for me. It's great fun and I have many friends among the competitors. My best friend, who is my age, also enjoys racing. During competitions, we both want to win, but afterward we get together to discuss our performances so that we help each other to improve.

I started taking part in competitions when I was six. I have now competed in more than 400 races and won more than a hundred medals and trophies. I am very proud of my world title for the 8-year-old

Felipe practicing his favorite sport.

junior category. During 1983, I competed in the experts' category in Holland, and came in sixth.

A BMX bicycle is made of special light material and weighs only 8 kilos (17½ lb). BMX races are extremely fast – each race lasts less than a minute. The secret of winning a race is to pedal all the time – this gives a few seconds' advantage. Trying to pedal around a curve is not as simple as it may seem and we have to be very careful, because it is easy to fall if the pedal touches the ground.

Even though I enjoy BMX racing so much, I am not fanatical about it. Our summers are very hot in Santiago – the temperature often reaches 35°C (95°F) – and I like to swim with friends in our pool, or watch TV. And I also enjoy athletics.

Felipe with some of the awards he has won for BMX racing.

"Archaeologists work like detectives"

Agustín Llagostera, 41, is married and has six children. He and his wife are archaeologists, working at San Pedro de Atacama Archaeological Museum, where Agustín is the Director.

Because of the extraordinary dryness of this area, organic matter does not disintegrate but just dehydrates (becomes very dry). This means that mummies over 20,000 years old, which have been found here, are in such good condition that it is

Agustín and his wife at the museum, working on a 2,000-year-old skeleton found on the site.

possible to study their internal organs and find out the cause of death. Doctors from many parts of the world come here to study the mummies in order to get a better understanding of present-day diseases — for example, to find out whether cancer existed in those far-off days and if so, how the disease has evolved.

The museum was founded twenty years

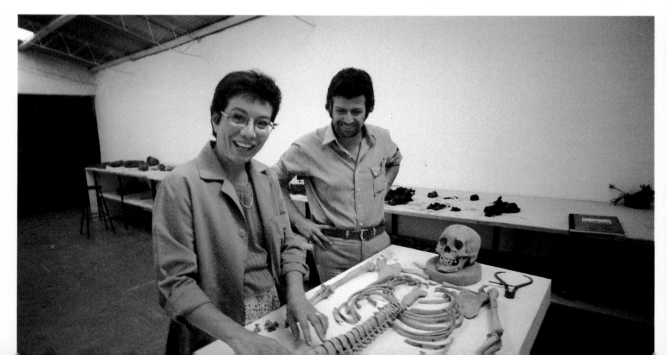

ago by the Dutch Jesuit Father Gustave Le Paige. He was a self-taught archaeologist with great intuition and determination. He discovered the archaeology of this area. The museum has more than 360,000 archaeological objects, ranging from arrows to mummies, almost all of them collected by Father Le Paige. I believe it is the biggest collection, on site, of any museum in the world.

This area is located near the Atacama Dry Salt Lake, where the Atacama culture flourished. Together with Bolivia, Peru and the north of Argentina, this area is known archaeologically as the "Andean Culture." San Pedro de Atacama is an oasis, situated on what was once an important road to the south, and to the coast. The Spanish conquerors went south, crossing the Atacama Desert along this road, and the oasis was a meeting place for people of various subcultures of the Andes Culture. All this makes the area very interesting archaeologically.

The museum plays an important part in the life of the native Indians of San Pedro de Atacama. They are able to see from our work here, that they have an ancient culture. It has helped them to regain a sense of identity and self-respect, which they and their ancestors lost when first the Spanish, and later their Chilean descendants, came to the region, imposing their own culture on the native Indians. Now the Indians realize that their ancestors had their own culture and identity, as valuable as ours, but different.

In addition to our international visitors, about 3,000 people come to see the museum during the summer months. I think this is a good number, considering

that we are 200 kilometers (124 miles) from Calama, and 300 kilometers (186 miles) from Antofagasta – the two nearest cities.

One of our biggest problems at the museum is that the tourists and traders who come here are often looking for souvenirs or objects that they can sell. These people destroy the serious investigation of archaeologists. Visitors are forbidden by law from doing their own excavations, but it is difficult to enforce this in such a large and isolated area.

The work of an archaeologist is similar to that of a detective. We constantly need to find new evidence to either support or disprove a theory.

The dramatic Licancabur Volcano rises behind Moon Valley, one of the driest places on earth, where almost nothing lives.

"One of the world's largest observatories"

Maria Teresa Ruiz, 37, is an astronomer. She is married and has a son. She and her husband work in the Department of Astronomy at the University of Chile. She has a doctorate from Princeton University, and has worked in Italy and Mexico.

The universe contains thousands and thousands of groups of galaxies. The Milky Way is part of one little group of galaxies, and our solar system is part of the Milky Way Galaxy. In our galaxy there are 1,001 stars similar to our sun, and any of these could have a solar system with an earth like ours.

Although our sun is similar to millions of other stars, as far as we know, it is the center of our planetary system. It is difficult for us to know about other planetary systems because we cannot easily see them. Planets do not give off light, they just reflect the light of a star (in the case of Earth, the light of the Sun).

Astronomers are trying to discover if one of the nearest stars to our solar system, Alpha Centauri, has a planetary system. This star is a distance of 4.3 light years away from Earth: one light year is the distance that light travels in a year.

My main interest at the moment is in the remnants of supernovas. These are exploding stars, and their remnants (remains) can tell us a lot about the composition of a star and about the universe.

Chile has excellent observation sites.

The CTIO main telescope is the largest in the southern hemisphere.

Near La Serena, 500 kilometers (310 miles) north of Santiago, there are three main international observatories. These constitute the largest collection of telescopes located in one region anywhere in the southern hemisphere. At Cerro Tololo, we have one of the world's largest observatories, the Inter-American Observatory (CTIO) situated 2,300 meters (7,546 feet) high on the slopes of the Andes. It has a four-meter telescope, the largest in the southern hemisphere.

Chilean astronomers can use these facilities free of charge, and we are the envy of other astronomers because, at Cerro Tololo, we can rely on having at least 300 clear nights every year.

I went to CTIO in 1968 when I was an engineering student. I had never been interested in astronomy before, but after my first visit I was captivated by the immensity of the universe, which I saw from Cerro Tololo. After that it was an easy decision for me to leave engineering

The Inter-American Observatory (CTIO), high up on the slopes of the Andes.

for astronomy. I became the first astronomer to obtain a degree from this department. I had to do two years' basic science, two years' physics, and two years' astronomy.

The Department of Astronomy at the University of Chile is located at Cerro Calan, in Santiago. We have our own telescopes, but we can only practice astrometrics (the branch of astronomy concerned with measuring stars, planets, etc.) because of the difficulties caused by city lights, humidity and smog.

At observatories like CTIO, astronomers don't watch directly through the telescopes. We work at the telescope computer terminal, analyzing the information received. The United States is planning to build its own terminal so that U.S. astronomers will not have to come to Chile for their observations.

"It is hard to live so far from my family"

Jorge Quezada, 30, works for the Chilean state-run petroleum industry, in the production department at Cullen Camp in Tierra del Fuego. His wife and son live in the nearest city, Punta Arenas.

Oil is found in Chile only in the Magellan Strait and in Tierra del Fuego (Land of Fire). This name was given to the southernmost tip of South America by the Spaniards, when they first discovered the area, because they saw huge bonfires which had been lit by the native Indians in order to keep themselves warm.

The search for oil has been going on from the beginning of the century. The first discovery was made at Cerro Sombrero, in Tierra del Fuego, in December 1945. Cerro Sombrero became an important camp, with all kinds of facilities for the oil workers. Nowadays, there is nothing left of the camp, but it has become an independent village, with all the public services of a small town, and it serves the community of sheep farmers who live in the region.

I work at Cullen, one of the many oil camps on Tierra del Fuego. I am in charge of the production of four oil wells. In this area, oil is obtained at very high pressures as a mixture of oil, water and gas. This mixture has to be separated and the gas and oil stored.

I work fifteen days at Cullen and then have five days' leave. I spend my leave with my wife and baby son, back in Punta Arenas. Although we have all the modern conveniences such as television, and the job is not difficult – except for the weather – it is hard to live so far from my family. So each time I get leave, I rush back to Punta Arenas, which is 270 kilometers (170 miles) away. During the winter, when the roads are icy, the journey can take up to eight hours. In summer, it only takes three hours.

Every two years I get fifty days' holiday, when we usually go to the north of Chile in search of a hot summer. Almost everybody from Punta Arenas does this. If we go by car, we have to drive across part of Argentina and enter Chile through Puyehue.

Because we are so far south, everything here is extremely expensive – for instance, fruit and vegetables have to be flown down

to us. For this reason, our salaries are very good compared with the rest of the country. When we go to Santiago, food, hotels and clothes seem very cheap to us, but imported goods are much cheaper here than in the capital because Punta Arenas is a free port.

Punta Arenas has the highest standard of living in Chile. Finding oil has helped, but unfortunately Magallanes – as the region is called – does not produce a lot of oil and can only supply 60 percent of the oil needed by Chile. The rest has to be imported. But oil explorations continue, especially in the Magellan Strait, where there are fifteen platforms in production.

Recently, deep-sea wells have been sunk to the south of Tierra del Fuego. Some have reached a depth of more than 4,000 meters (13,000 feet).

Cerro Sombrero camp, which is now an independent village on Tierra del Fuego.

Jorge working the "Christmas tree" valves at an oil well.

"Pisco is our national drink"

Sigifredo Gonzalez, age 55, is foreman at the Pisco Control Distillery in La Serena. The distillery is the biggest producer of pisco in Chile.

I was born in Coquimbo, which is 10 kilometers (6 miles) south of La Serena. I work in a pisco distillery in the grape-producing region near La Serena. Pisco is our national drink, and is similar to brandy.

Pisco was discovered by chance nearly 130 years ago, when muscat grapes were brought from Spain, with the idea of producing wine in the Elqui Valley, 90 kilometers (56 miles) from La Serena. The hot climate in the valley all year round, combined with clear skies for more than 300 days a year, low rainfall and very little wind, produced grapes with a high sugar content. With the limited techniques of those days, it was difficult to preserve the wine made from these sweet grapes. So the producers, trying to save their produce, decided to distill the wine, and they named the product of their distillation "pisco." The result was so successful that pisco is still obtained from the distillation of wine from muscat grapes, which is not suitable for drinking otherwise.

Pisco is a transparent spirit with a distinctive flavor and aroma which brings to mind the sunny valleys where the grapes grow and mature.

At La Serena, we distill pisco from wine produced in the Elqui and Limari Valleys. Pisco produced in other parts of Chile is slightly different — ours is the authentic pisco!

The wine arrives at La Serena with a high alcoholic grade. Here it is stored in casks and vats made of American oak for the process of maturing, which takes from six to twelve months. After that period it is diluted into the various commercial alcholic grades. Then it is bottled and distributed around the country.

During the last five years we have been exporting pisco to other countries in South America and to some countries in Europe.

Pisco of a low alcoholic grade is very popular for mixing with soft drinks like Coca Cola, or for preparing the popular "pisco sour," which is four parts pisco to one part lemon juice, sugar and lots of ice.

I have been working here for the last eighteen years. Our distillery is a co-operative, established in 1931 with nine original members. Nowadays there are more than 400 members. The total production of muscat grapes from the Elqui and Limari Valleys comes to our distilleries. We produce 50 percent of the pisco in Chile, processing more than 33 tons of muscat grapes. We produce other spirits too, based on apricots and various fruits.

The main difference between pisco and wine, apart from the alcoholic grade, is that, because of the special process of distillation, pisco does not vary in quality from year to year. It always has the same bouquet and aroma, no matter what the vintage.

Below: *Inside the pisco distillery.*

"I believe fish have intelligence"

Alejandro Flores, 29, is married and has one daughter. In 1983, at Antofagasta, he became World Champion of underwater hunting. He earns his living by fishing with his harpoon. His wife helps him to sell his catch at the fish market at Antofagasta.

The waters of the Pacific Ocean at this latitude (23° south of the Equator) are moderately warm and transparent. They provide excellent conditions for underwater fishing.

We form teams of three or four scubadivers, and hunt together in the same area, in order to reduce the cost of transportation to different places around the coast. It is unwise to hunt for many days in one particular area, because the fish will disappear. This may sound strange, but I believe that fish have intelligence, and they know when we are going to kill them. Many times I have gone underwater without my harpoon to try to understand their habits and learn more of their environment. This knowledge helps me later, when I'm hunting. When I am observing them, the fish watch me but they don't swim away. But when I go down with my harpoon, they immediately vanish.

It's not unusual for scubadivers to hear the sounds that some fish make underwater. The conger eel, for example, sounds like a frog. We develop a strange sense when we're underwater, and can "hear" a fish moving. If we turn around, we invariably find that the fish is in the spot where

Alejandro with his awards as a champion underwater hunter.

we "heard" it.

We go underwater without oxygen tanks. I have a very fast reoxygenation power that allows me, in less than a minute, to be ready to go down again. This makes me a very fast hunter. I like to work at a depth of 20 to 25 meters (65 to 82 feet). The bigger fish are found at this depth, but I only have a minute to find and kill a fish. I try to hit it in the head and kill it instantly. If the harpoon misses the fatal place, the injured fish can move very fast. Usually I am only a meter away, at the end of the harpoon, and sometimes, when it is trying to escape, a fish may hit me with the harpoon, or get me entangled in the harpoon rope. In this situation, an underwater hunter must have strong nerves and stay calm.

If the weather conditions are good, and they are for most of the year in Antofagasta, I work from Monday to Friday. My usual daily catch is 80 kilograms (176 lb), or forty or fifty fish, which constitutes nearly five hours' work.

In 1983, I won the World Championship for underwater hunting. The competition lasted two days. The first day I was far behind the leader, and only my fast recovery power, allowing me to be ready for the next dive, enabled me to win on the second day. During the championship I caught 161 kilograms (335 lb) of fish. I received medals and cups after winning the world title.

The Humboldt Current from the Antarctic flows along our coast, giving our waters a low temperature. During 1982, the temperature of the sea went up from 18°C to 24°C (64°F to 75°F). All the seaweed and molluscs along the coast north of La Serena were killed. Recovery has been slow, but seaweed is now reappearing on the rocks. Up to now, nobody has been able to give a satisfactory explanation for that warm current.

Antofagasta harbor where Alejandro sells his catch at the fish market.

"The sensation of skiing is wonderful"

Sergio Correa, 28, works as a ski instructor at Antillanca in the Andes Mountains. The Andes mountain range forms Chile's natural eastern limit with Argentina and Bolivia.

I started skiing at the age of 22, when I was a student of physics at the University of Osorno. Free ski classes were being offered at Antillanca, and I decided to have a try. From the first day I loved it and quickly realized that I wanted to specialize as a ski instructor. With a lot of effort and working really hard all through each season, I became a ski instructor after only three years. This is not a long training, I know, but fortunately I have a natural ability for skiing.

I now work as a ski instructor for the Osorno Ski Club, and spend almost all the season, from May to September, up in the mountains. At Antillanca there are many ski schools, full of students learning the sport. The most important ski resort is Portillo, 160 kilometers (100 miles) north of Santiago. Portillo was the site of the 1966 World Ski Championships. It was chosen because of its good race tracks, well-known among professionals.

The most popular ski resort for Chileans is Farellones, only 40 kilometers (25

miles) from Santiago, where all the people from the capital go for their skiing. Farther south there are other resorts. At Punta Arenas, the slopes are only fifteen minutes from the city. It is the only place on this continent where it is possible to see the sea while skiing.

Because Punta Arenas is so far south, the surrounding hills are covered with snow for five or six months of the year. In spite of our facilities, Chileans are not very enthusiastic about skiing. The skiing tradition is relatively new to the country. The sport is very expensive in Chile, but more and more people are learning, which pleases me. I really would like to see more people skiing. The sensation of gliding over snow on a sunny day, with a deep blue sky overhead, and just the swoosh of skis on the snow, is wonderful.

The Andes determine the character of Chilean geography. The mountains are a natural eastern border between Chile and Argentina and Bolivia. They run from north to south for almost 4,000 kilometers

Right: *The ski slopes at Punta Arenas, overlooking the Magellan Straits and Tierra del Fuego.*

(2,500 miles). The Aconcagua peak near Santiago is one of the highest mountains in the world.

Chile is a long and narrow country with an average width of 150 kilometers (93 miles). When we look east we can see the Andes from almost everywhere in the country. To the west we always see the Pacific Ocean.

The Andes give geographical characteristics to Chile that are different from Bolivia's or Argentina's. In Chile, the north is mostly desert and extremely dry, whereas Bolivia and Argentina, on the other side of the mountains, have tropical jungle. In the south, Chile has heavy rainfall and the land is densely forested.

Below: *Waiting to go up on the lift to the top of the ski slopes at Atillanca.*

"I dance to honor the Virgin"

José Ormeño, 35, is married and has one son. He earns his living as a shoemaker in Iquique, his home town. He is the *caporal*, or leader, of a dance group that honors the Virgin of the Carmen at the annual Festival of La Tirana, in the Atacama Desert.

I started dancing twenty-four years ago, after a Bolivian dance group visited us for the annual festival of La Tirana. Our group is known as *La Endiablada de la Virgen Del Carmen* (The Devils of the Virgin of the Carmen), and our members are called *diablos* (devils).

Ten years ago our dance leader died, and I was elected to take his place. As *caporal* (dance leader), I direct the figures that the dancers perform, conducting with my hands and with a whistle.

Each dance group has its own band. There are twenty-two musicians in *La Endiablada:* seven trumpets, five trombones, two cymbals and eight drums. The musicians do not dance, but remain in the middle of the group, where they can be heard by everyone.

We have fifty men and forty women in our group. Each of the performers has three or four handmade costumes, made from any color and material they choose. We design our costumes especially to honor the Virgin. I have more than eight costumes and I wear them all at different times during the Festival.

All the dancers and musicians come here either to honor the Virgin or to fulfill

José and a friend in their costumes for the La Tirana festival.

a promise made to her in return for a favor granted. For years I danced for the Virgin, fulfilling promises made to her. Now that I have completed these promises, I dance simply to honor her.

The groups begin arriving in the small village of La Tirana on July 13, the first day of the Festival. The village has a population of 5,000 and is situated in the middle of the *Pampa del Tamarugal*, near the Atacama Desert, 70 kilometers (43 miles) from Iquique, where I live. During the festival, the population increases to 150,000 devoted pilgrims.

First, the dancers go to the Calvary Cross, at the entrance to the village. There, we receive a blessing from the priests and then we start dancing through the main street toward the sanctuary. We dance for three days, in honor of the Virgin. All this time we do not drink alcohol or take any other stimulants. By the end of the third day we are exhausted and it is only our faith that keeps us dancing.

The village was named La Tirana, meaning tyrant, because an Indian princess of the region was once converted to Catholicism by her Spanish lover. Having been converted, she became a tyrant, trying to impose the Catholic faith on her people by force. The people rose up in anger against the couple, and killed them.

Many years later, a priest built a small sanctuary to the Virgin of the Carmen, in memory of the princess and her lover. People began coming each year to pray to the Virgin, and this tradition has been maintained ever since.

In my family, my father, grandfather and great-grandfather have all honored the Virgin. Now my son, who has begun dancing with our group, has also chosen to continue the tradition.

Caporal José Ormeño inside his shoe store.

"Ideal conditions for growing pine trees"

Aroldo Sepulveda, 26, is married and has a six-month-old baby. He works as a woodcutter in the forests around Concepción. He began working in the forests with his father, at the age of 8.

Concepción is the second most important industrial city in Chile, after Santiago. It is 500 kilometers (300 miles) south of the capital and only 20 kilometers (12 miles) from the Pacific Ocean. It has

Oxen are used to drag the felled timber.

big port facilities for the steel and chemical industries, fisheries and mines, all of which give work to thousands of people in the region.

But the huge pine forests are the main characteristic of the area. These supply the raw materials for the paper industry and timber for the national and international markets. The export of timber and

cellulose is the second most important source of money to the country.

The heavy rainfall and sandy soil of the region provide ideal conditions for the growing of pine trees. Conditions are so good that after only fifteen years, trees are ready to be used in the production of cellulose, which is the raw material for the production of paper. Near here there are four big cellulose factories, two of them producing cellulose only for the international market.

A few years ago I worked for one of these factories, in its own large forest, but now I prefer to work independently. At present I work near Concepción, with a contractor who buys small forests and sells the timber. I can spend more time with my family, and am able to sleep at home. I couldn't do this when I worked for the big companies, as I would spend more than a month at a time away from my family.

I am now working in a small, fifteen-year-old pine forest with about 5,000 young trees, only 10 kilometers (6 miles) from my home. I usually walk through the countryside to work, or I may get a lift in a truck. I am used to walking a lot so I don't find it tiring.

We work from the beginning of September, when the six-month-long season starts. With eight men, it takes two months to complete the work. Each of us has very specific jobs. As I own a motor saw, I am in charge of cutting down the trees. I have three men under me. Two have axes, and they chop the branches off the fallen tree and mark the trunk so that I can cut it into blocks. The other man, with the help of two trained oxen, drags the tree trunks to trucks. These will transport the timber to the big saw mills which buy the produce of all the small timber contractors.

Oxen are more economical than tractors

Aroldo at work in the forest.

for a small forest like this. The animals have tremendous strength and can drag up to a ton in weight. If they are properly looked after, they can work for fifteen years or longer.

I've been cutting down trees for more than ten years. Although I don't consider myself an expert, I can fell a tree so that it falls exactly where I want it to. I have learned with practice, patience and great care, to fell a tree with my motor saw. First I make a horizontal cut in the middle of the tree at a distance of 15 or 20 centimeters (6 to 8 inches) from the ground, on the side where I want it to fall. About 10 to 20 centimeters (4 to 8 inches) above I start another cut, at an angle so that it joins up with the first cut, in the middle of the trunk. The angle of the wedge will determine where the tree will fall. Then I make a third cut on the opposite side of the trunk. With this last cut I have complete control over the direction of the falling tree. The entire operation takes no more than two minutes.

"The driest place on Earth"

Carlos Peralta is a wagon driver at the Maria Elena nitrate mine, in the Atacama Desert. This is one of only two nitrate workings left in Chile, now that synthetic nitrate has replaced natural nitrate as a fertilizer.

Large-scale nitrate production developed during the second half of the nineteenth century, when this area belonged partly to Peru and partly to Bolivia. In 1879 Peru and Bolivia fought a war against Chile, because the Chileans were exploiting the nitrate in the region. In those days, nitrate production was big business, so much so that it was called "white gold."

During that period, there were more than sixty nitrate mines in the Atacama Desert, with nearly 15,000 workers. It is said that huge tracts of the desert were lit up at night by the fires from the smelting furnaces.

The production of nitrate lasted until synthetic nitrates were invented by the Germans during the first world war. Synthetic nitrate is obtained through a chemical process based on nitrogen, and is much cheaper to produce than natural nitrate. It also has the advantage of not being dependent on territorial boundaries.

Now, silence and darkness have returned to the Atacama Desert, which is littered with abandoned nitrate mines waiting for better times. Perhaps in the future, the fate of the nitrate mines may change, for scientists have reported that synthetic nitrate "burns" the soil after many years of use.

I work in one of the last working nitrate mines in Chile. It is called Maria Elena and was built in 1929. This and one other (the Pedro de Valvidia) are the only nitrate sites still operating, twenty-four hours a day, supplying the world with natural nitrate through the port of Ocopilla, 80 kilometers (50 miles) away. Both nitrate mines are state-owned.

Nitrate is found on the surface of the Atacama Desert. It forms a crust or "caliche" up to a depth of 2 meters (6½ feet). Deep holes are drilled in the caliche, one meter (3 feet) apart. These are filled with dynamite which, when exploded, loosens the soil so that the caliche can be easily removed. This is then taken by train to the mill.

I drive a wagon which is winched up

Right: *One of the wagons which Carlos has to drive every day.*

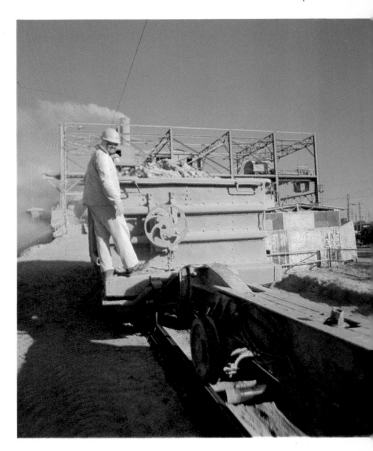

to the mill. Here, the wagon is filled with soil and caliche. It is then emptied and the process repeated. The caliche is separated from the soil, and heated so that the nitrate floats. To protect ourselves from the very fine dust of the caliche, which could get into our lungs and cause silicosis, we have to wear respirator masks.

I work from 3:00 in the afternoon until 11:00 at night. Toward the end of my shift the *camachaca* (sea fog) descends. This is a dangerous time, because the fog makes everything slippery and it is easy to fall and be caught by machinery.

The Atacama Desert is the driest place on earth. There has been practically no rain here for hundreds of years. Mine is a very hard job — working always in dust and wind. It is very hot during the day and very cold at night. If I ever had the opportunity, I would like to work somewhere else.

Below: *A truck loaded with nitrate.*

"I prefer to live in the country"

Bruni Dietz, 34, is the mother of four children. Her husband is a farmer, and they live in the countryside, 25 kilometers (15 miles) from Osorno.

My ancestors came to this area from Hessen, in Germany, after the Chilean government invited Europeans from England, Germany, France and Switzerland to colonize the south of Chile. A lot of German people came, mainly because the climate of Germany is similar to this part of Chile. Many old houses in Osorno have a German style of architecture, as have some of the old farmhouses in the region.

When colonization began, around 1860, the area was populated by Mapuche Indians, who never accepted the white man, and never surrendered to the Spaniards. Those were difficult times for the settlers, who had to contend with both the Indians and the weather, which is very wet.

The region was heavily forested and for many years the production of timber was the main activity of the region. Slowly, the forests were cut down, giving place to open areas where grass could be grown for cattle. Nowadays, the main activity is cattle raising and milk production.

The soil here is very good. Grass is undoubtedly our best crop, but other products, such as potatoes, beets, oats and

Bruni's husband, Hernan, repairing his tractor which has broken down and has to be pulled by oxen.

rape are also grown. Apples are the most common fruit. From them we make cider, which is a very popular drink in the region. On our farm we have apple trees, and my husband sows potatoes and beets. I have my own small garden, with fresh vegetables for the family and fruit trees for jam.

Our farm is located in the Central Valley. To the east are the Andes and to the west the Coastal Mountains and Pacific Ocean. But temperatures are lower here than on the coast, and we have much more rain.

This area is known as "The Region of the Lakes," because there are so many lakes of different sizes. During the summer we often spend a day at Puyehue Lake and have tea in one of the many cafés around the shore and near the international road into Argentina. This road is very important as it is the only way to get to Punta Arenas, in the south of Chile. There is a good ski resort called Antillanca, in the Andes Mountains, not far away. There is a fantastic view from up there. The coast is only 50 kilometers (31 miles) from Osorno, and there are two beautiful and fully-equipped hot-spring resorts not far away.

Even though the rainfall is so heavy, I wouldn't change where we live for any place in the world, not even Santiago. I prefer to live in the country.

Unfortunately, we will have to move to Osorno soon because of our children's education. At the moment we take turns with other parents to drive them to Osorno. But the long journey is tiring for them and they miss a lot of school. Although there are good boarding schools at Osorno — I went to the German boarding school there — I don't want my children to board. I believe children should spend as much time as possible at home with their parents.

Old wooden houses in Osorno, with German-influenced architecture.

"We are very proud of our crafts"

Elisardo Madrid, 26, is married and has two children. He was born at Chimbarango and has lived there all his life. Like most of the other villagers, he works with osier, or willow, with which he manufactures furniture and ornaments.

Almost everybody in Chimbarongo is employed making furniture from osier, or willow. This industry has made our village famous. An osier chair or table from Chimbarongo is noted for its high quality and low cost. If well-treated, one of our chairs can last for ten years.

Apart from furniture, we manufacture ornaments, such as animals, for the house or garden. The most popular of these are elephants, which are 50 centimeters (19 inches) high, and also birds. I really don't know why people like elephants so much, because there are no elephants in Chile, or America, for that matter. Maybe it's because there aren't any that they are so popular!

I have been working with osiers since I was a child. Like many homes in Chimbarongo, we have our own osier plantation behind the house. We have planted a quarter of a hectare (half an acre) but this is not enough to meet all our requirements, and we have to buy more supplies of osier from other producers.

To use the osier, the bark must first be peeled from it, and then it is divided into four long strips. From each of these strips thinner strips are obtained, with a special tool called a laminator. The strips are wetted and are then ready to be used.

I sell my products mainly to a merchant who specializes in selling goods from Chimbarongo in his shop in Santiago. We are lucky to be only one kilometer (about half a mile) from the Pan American Highway, the most important road in Chile, which carries a lot of traffic. This road runs from Puerto Montt, in Chile, to Alaska, in the United States, and provides a road link for all the countries of America. We have stands beside the Highway, and are able to sell our products to passing tourists.

Since the last century, people in this area have worked the osier to make their own furniture and other useful items, such as baskets. The long and narrow geography of Chile has produced areas with many different crafts, and we are very

44

Craftsmen and women at work during the Annual Crafts Fair held at Santiago.

proud of our country craft traditions. For example, the typical woolen socks and sweaters of Chiloé, in the south; the carpets of the Mapuche Indians of Temuco; the carved wooden flowers of Villarrica and the small stone churches of the north. But my favorite is the craft of Rari, a little village near here. The women of Rari make small figures — people, animals, butterflies, rings, earrings, and so on out of horsehair. They make strong dyes using a secret process, and dye the hairs with beautiful, permanent colors. Then they patiently braid the hairs, fashioning them into figures. These are very beautiful and require a great deal of skill.

During the first two weeks in December, an annual craft fair is held in Santiago. This is an excellent way of seeing nearly all the examples of Chilean craftsmanship. The fair has grown very much in recent years, and many countries of Latin America are well represented there. It is a fascinating place to visit and see good craftsmanship.

Elisardo showing his young brother how to use the laminator which splits the osiers.

"The trees produce two crops a year"

Enrique Arroyo, 45, is married and has three children. He was born at Pica, where he works as manager at the state-owned Esmeralda fruit farm. The farm, in addition to growing fruit, provides technical advice to local farmers.

The Esmeralda Fruit Farm is situated in the middle of the Atacama Desert. At this point the desert is rich in underground water that filters down from the Andes Mountains. The land here is desert because it is situated between the Chilean coast – along which flows the cold Humboldt Current – and the high Andes Mountains. Clouds forming over the Pacific condense into rain over the Humboldt Current, leaving the land below the Andes free from rain. As the clouds rise over the mountains they condense again in the cool air and rain falls on the mountain slopes.

The desert climate and the underground waters provide ideal conditions for the tamarugo tree, which gives its name to this part of the desert – *la Pampa del Tamargual*. The tamarugo seeds are protected by a pod, similar to but bigger than a peanut. These make very good animal feed.

Fifteen people work at this farm, all of them from nearby Pica, 10 kilometers (6 miles) away. Pica is an oasis which has been inhabited since ancient times. I work here from 7:30 a.m. to 7:30 p.m. from Monday to Friday, supervising the work of the farm.

When nitrate was worked extensively in the desert at the turn of the century,

Enrique with some of his giant grapefruit.

Pica provided fruit and vegetables for the workers. Nowadays the oasis has greatly increased its production of fruits, mainly oranges, lemons and grapefruit. We also grow mangoes, dates, avocados and tomatoes.

The climate here remains the same throughout the year. We have an average temperature of 33°C (91°F) and low humidity which makes the high temperatures bearable.

This climate means that the fruit trees produce two crops per year. Because the trees are planted at different periods, it is possible to have citrus fruits all year round. We have more than six varieties of grapefruit, some weighing more than a kilo (2.2 lb) each. This may sound impressive, but they are not a very commercial product. We are now directing our efforts to producing fruits which are resistant to pests and which travel well. Sweetness and juiciness are important too.

Occasionally the fruit is affected by

La Pampa del Tamarugal *in the middle of the Atacama Desert, where the oasis is situated.*

pests. Some years ago it was attacked by a type of bluefly (or fruit fly) that came from Peru. The flies laid their eggs inside the fruit, producing maggots that ate the fruit. All the crops at Pica and other nearby oases were totally ruined. Although we managed to exterminate the pest, unfortunately other insects were destroyed as well, upsetting the ecological balance at the oasis. We have had to go to Tacna, in Peru, to bring back replacements for the insects that were lost.

Although we have not been affected since, there are strict controls to make sure that the bluefly does not come back. Any fruit that is transported from one part of Chile to another is carefully inspected to make sure it is free of pests. Thus we avoid the risk of introducing disease to the central region of the country, where most Chilean fruit is produced.

"Talca folklore is famous"

Hector Escalona is 39 and married and has four children. He is a disc jockey at a radio station in Talca. He also sings regional folk songs, accompanying himself on his guitar. Talca and the surrounding region is famous for its folklore, which is deeply rooted in Chilean traditions.

Chile is a country with a very rich folklore that varies from north to south. Folklore is the unwritten literature of a people, expressed in stories, songs, proverbs, dances, and so on.

In the north, the folklore is strongly influenced by Bolivia. The people dress in bright colors, which they never normally see in the surrounding desert, and their music is joyful. They play mainly wind instruments such as *quenas*, flutes, whistles and *zampoñas*: or stringed instruments like the *charango*. This is a tiny guitar, made from the shell of the charango, a small creature living in the Atacama Desert.

Coming south to the Central Zone, Talca folklore is famous. During the season, many rodeos and cowboy shows are held throughout the region. The wine, which is our national drink, is delicious and is produced in large quantities. Typical Chilean food, like *empanadas* (meat pies) and *asados a la parrilla* (barbecued steak) with Chilean salad, can be eaten anywhere. The region of the Central Zone is very typical of Chile and most of the population live here, between Santiago and Los Angeles. The weather is sunny, the humidity is

Hector in his office at the radio station, where he works as a disc jockey.

normal, and the winters are mild.

The folklore of the Central Zone is typically Chilean, inherited from the traditions brought here by the Spanish conquerors, and adapted to the country and its native traditions. The *cueca*, our national dance, is performed by everyone in Talca. It is a courtship dance between a man and a woman. During the dance, the man tries to capture the lady, and eventually succeeds.

The main work in the Central Zone is agriculture. For centuries, good harvests have been celebrated by dancing and music. This is the root of our folklore. The musical instruments we use most are the guitar, accompanied by harp and accordion.

Going south, the folklore gradually changes, becoming very different at the island of Chiloé, where the Spanish influence has only slightly affected the ancient mythology and traditions of the native Indians. Here the people also dance the *cueca*, but the music is typical of the Indian people.

Farther south, we arrive at Coyhaique, where the folklore is a mixture of both Chiloé and the Central Zone, brought by natives of these regions when they settled here, barely fifty years ago. At Punta Arenas and Tierra del Fuego, the regional folklore has a strong Argentinian influence.

My family has always been involved with music. I play the guitar and sing under the professional name of Don Jacinto, in memory of my grandfather, who was a famous folk singer. My eldest son also plays the guitar and is becoming a good folk singer. I am very proud of him.

I work as a disc jockey at a radio station at Talca, on one of the three Chilean music programs that are broadcast daily. I also lead a group of musicians, and as a folk singer, I interpret the different music and traditions of the region. My costume represents a Chilean peasant of the Central Zone.

Hector chats with his father who manufactures handmade saddles.

"The ideal climate for producing wine"

Ignacio Recabarren, 35, is married and has four children. For the last seven years he has worked as wine taster at Vina Santa Rita, in the Maipo Valley, where the most important Chilean vineyards are located.

The ideal climate for a wine-producing region has warm summers, which allow the grapes to mature slowly; rain-free autumns for a good harvest; moderate winters, so that the vines can develop; and

Ignacio in the bottling department at the vineyard.

finally, a mild spring with no frosts — which would destroy the young vines. All these conditions are found in what is known as a "Mediterranean climate," which exists in only a very few parts of the world. In Chile, this "Mediterranean" climate occurs in the central region of the country, particularly in the valley of the

River Maipo.

Chile holds an important place among the winemakers of the world, but outside South America, Chilean wines are not well-known. This is partly because our marketing policies are poorly organized and also the cost of transporting the wines abroad makes them very expensive and uncompetitive.

Producing good quality wines began in Chile as a hobby for the rich during the nineteenth century. For many years, these people were only concerned with improving the quality of the wine and not with expanding the industry.

Our vineyard is the second oldest in the country. It was started in 1880, with vines brought from France by members of an ancient, rich Chilean family. The vineyard suffered the same problems as others of the period, resulting in low production and policies of non-expansion.

Nowadays our attitudes have completely changed. We are retaining the quality of the wines but are expanding at the same time, and trying hard to reach international markets, especially the United States and Europe.

Since 1982, we have greatly increased production, and with new equipment we are now able to bottle 10,000 bottles an hour, working twenty hours a day. We have 25 million liters of wine stored in our cellars.

Cork is vital to the life of wine. A poor quality cork will contaminate the wine, giving it a different flavor, or it can let air into the bottle, which will ruin it. A good cork allows the wine to keep for years.

Chilean wines are very cheap. Our best wine, bottled under the name "Casa Real" is sold at 300 pesos (about $1.75). This wine won the 1983 Double Gold Medal, in Great Britain, for the best Cabernet-Sauvignon – chosen from 800 wines from all over the world. I am very proud of this award, for as chief wine taster, it is my responsibility to give our wines their unique character.

We have 150 hectares (370 acres) at Maipo valley, producing the grapes for our best quality wines. For our cheaper varieties, we buy the grapes from other smaller vineyards which grow grapes exclusively for us.

Because of our special soil characteristics, a two-year-old wine in Chile is similar to a four-year-old wine produced in Europe. This means we do not need to store our wines as long as other wine-producing countries.

The vineyards in the Maipo valley have to be kept clear of weeds – this is done by a horse-drawn weeder, guided by hand.

"Chileans are not fond of eating fish"

Eleodoro Mendez, 42, is married and has two children. He came to Iquique to work as a crew member on a small fishing boat, in the early sixties. Now he is an experienced skipper commanding a 300-ton fishing vessel, with ten crew members.

When I arrived at Iquique twenty years ago, the fishing industry was just beginning. In those days there were only a few small boats of no more than 50 tons. People from all over Chile were moving here to live, and in a couple of years the fishing industry had expanded enormously. There were shipyards, and more than twenty businesses, specializing in fishing for anchovies. As the industry grew, our experience also grew, and many of us were able to become skippers.

In 1967, the anchovies disappeared from our coasts. The industry collapsed and the shipyards closed. Those were hard times, but the fishing industry adapted. We had been used to working only during the day, but after the anchovies disappeared we started working at night and, with more sophisticated instruments and larger vessels, we got better results. Nowadays we catch mainly sardine and jurel. After a few years the industry recovered, making Iquique the most important fishing port in the country, with a fleet of nearly a hundred fishing boats.

It is not difficult to find fish during the night because a shoal gives a phosphorescent light on the water. It is possible to determine which kind of fish we have ahead of us. For instance, jurel show as a reddish tint on the water and sardine give purple and dark green colors. If there are any anchovies, they show as a purple color.

As skipper, I decide when to throw the nets. This is a vital movement, requiring a lot of experience. The ideal way to make a catch is to get as near as possible to the fish in one throw. If I fail, we get few fish, which means more work, trying to get the nets back into the boat again for another throw; or too much fish, which is very dangerous because the catch could weigh so much that it drags the boat down to the bottom. After more than twenty years at sea, I have learned to respect it. If we are not careful the sea can be very dangerous.

Our monthly catch is about 3,000 tons of fish, during an average of twenty days

at sea. During 1982, a total of 3,500,000 tons of fish was caught off the coasts of Chile, of which 1,500,000 tons were caught by the Iquique fleet. Chileans do not enjoy eating fish – they prefer meat – so most of the catch is turned into fish flour, which is exported for fertilizer and animal feed. Chile is the world's major producer of fish flour.

It is important for us to catch as much fish as possible. We earn a basic salary and get a percentage for each ton of fish we catch. As skipper, I receive three times as much as the crew. I have ten men under my command – engineer, mate, cook and *panguero*, who is in charge of the little net boat, and six crew members.

Below: *Fishing boats in the port of Iquique.*

"The city is full of history"

Carmencita Ponce is married and has four children. She lives at Chillán, where she teaches history and geography at a secondary school. She and her husband come from Valparaiso, in the north.

Chillán has a population of 100,000. It is the birthplace of many Chilean national figures – so much so that the city has been referred to as "the cradle of heroes and artists." Our liberator from the Spanish rulers and first president of the newly-born Republic of Chile, Bernardo O'Higgins, was born in Chillán, as were many other important people in our history, including the world-famous pianist, Claudio Arrau. The city is full of history.

I teach history and geography at Public School No. 1, which was built in 1853. It used to be a large boarding school for the children of people living in the countryside around the city, because there were no schools in the villages. But nowadays, nearly all the villages in Chile have at least an elementary school, and so parents have stopped using boarding schools for their young children.

The school now has 2,000 day pupils, averaging thirty to a class. I teach the thirteen- and fourteen-year-olds two hours of Chilean history and two hours of Chilean geography each week. I also take other classes, where I teach world geography and history. This is now a boys' school, although at one time it was intended to

Schoolboys in the school playground during the midday recess.

make it coeducational. However, this didn't happen, and I am glad, because I prefer to teach boys rather than girls – it seems to me that boys get better marks in history and geography than girls, although I suppose this wasn't so in my case!

My husband – who is also a teacher – and I came to Chillán twenty-five years ago. We came from Valparaiso, 500 kilometers (310 miles) to the north, on the Pacific coast. I studied at the Catholic University of Valparaiso, specializing in history and geography. We still miss our home town. Chillán, located on the slopes of the Andes, is cold in winter and hot in summer. During the day, in summer, the temperatures reach 35°C, dropping during the night to 15°C (95°F to 59°F). I have never adapted to this abrupt change of temperature.

Chillán has some advantages, being so near the Andes. There is a big ski resort with hot springs only 70 kilometers (43 miles) from the town. It is a beautiful place and people go there from Concepción, Los Angeles and Talca. As the snow lasts one month longer than at Santiago, skiers come there for the final snows of the winter.

The region around Chillán is mainly agricultural, for it is part of the Central Zone. The town is surrounded by farms and villages which provide agricultural produce for sale in Chillán.

Farmers and peasants come every day to the market in Chillán, which is very important and is considered to be one of the best markets in Chile. The regional crafts shops and stalls are famous throughout the country. It is also famous for its food. Some of the best Chilean dishes can be eaten here, in the small restaurants in the market. People particularly enjoy *cazuela de pava* (turkey soup), which is the best in the country.

Carmencita with her pupils.

"This area used to be in Bolivia"

Luis Yori, 28, is married and has two daughters. He is at present assigned to the International Police at the Chucuyo customs post, high up in the Altiplano, near the Bolivian border.

Our police force was created in 1927. To begin with there were only men in the force, but nowadays women are also being recruited.

I entered the force when I was nineteen and worked in Arica for a couple of years. Then I was assigned to the International Police at Chacalluta, the Chilean custom post at the border with Peru in the extreme north of the country. For the last fifteen months I have been working in the interior – the Altiplano – at the Chucuyo customs post near the border with Bolivia.

Up here, life can be hard, away from our families and friends. Although the scenery of the Altiplano is very impressive, I find that it becomes monotonous after a few months. The nights are bitterly cold and during the day there is always a cold wind blowing. The altitude – 4,000 meters (13,120 feet) – makes us tire more quickly than we would at sea level.

After thirty days' duty we have five days' leave at Arica with our families. I usually go to the beach with my wife and children when I'm on leave. The ideal climate of Arica makes it possible to do this all the year round.

At Chucuyo, the International Police check drivers' licenses and their vehicles

Luis at the barrier of the Chucuyo customs post at the frontier with Bolivia.

Luis checks a Bolivian truck on its way from Bolivia to the Chilean port of Arica.

and police records, if any. Passports and visas, needed by people entering or leaving the country, are dealt with by customs officers. There is also an officer dealing with the transportation of fruit, vegetables and animals in or out of the country.

I work a 24-hour shift and I am in charge of checking drivers' documents and their political records, in case they are not permitted to enter the country. After my shift, I have 24 hours free, when I may help with odd jobs if needed, or I just sleep.

Before the war of 1879 between Chile and Bolivia, this area, the "Chilean" Altiplano, used to be in Bolivia, and the port of Arica was in Peru. Because of its controversial history, there is still sometimes conflict in this area, which is of great strategic importance to Chile, because from here water is pumped to Arica and

its valleys.

In the old days, this area of the country used to be part of the Incan Empire, which was divided when the Spaniards came. This is why the cultures of the Chilean and Bolivian natives are so similar.

Because Bolivia is an inland country, without a port, there is a lot of truck traffic from Arica. The Bolivian government has special facilities at the port and receives special tax concessions for its goods.

Our busiest days at the customs post are Tuesdays and Fridays, when apart from the trucks, buses between Arica and La Paz pass through.

Facts

Capital City: Santiago, population 4,039 million (1982).

Principal language: Spanish, although several Indian dialects are still spoken in isolated areas.

Currency: The Chilean peso. 193 pesos = $1.

Religion: 82 percent of the population is Roman Catholic. 9 percent is Protestant, living mainly in the major cities.

Population: (1982) 11.49 million. Approximately 73 percent of the population live in Central Chile, the north and extreme south of the country being very sparsely populated due to the climate.

Climate: The north of Chile is mostly desert. The Atacama Desert is the driest place on earth with very few people living there. The central region of the country, around Santiago and Valparaiso, enjoys a Mediterranean climate with mild winters and very warm summers. Most of the country's agriculture is carried on in this area. To the south of this region the climate is very wet and the land densely forested. Cattle and sheep farming is carried out in areas where the forest has been cut down.

Government: Chile became a republic, independent from Spain, in 1819. In 1973, following a coup, the government was taken over by a military junta led by General Pinochet. The junta outlawed the Marxist party and assumed widespread powers. In 1978 a new constitution was elected by 67.5 percent of the population of Chile. This came into force in 1981, providing a return to democracy after a minimum period of 8 years, during which time General Pinochet would remain in control of the government. At the end of this period, a single successor would be appointed by the junta.

Education: There are three levels of education in Chile; elementary, secondary and university. Elementary education is free and has been compulsory since 1920. Public expenditure on education is among the highest of all South American countries. There are eight universities in Chile.

Industry: Most of Chilean industry is found in and around Santiago and Valparaiso. Chile is virtually self-sufficient in iron and steel production with tin plate and copper being produced in large quantities. The export trade is dominated by minerals, with copper, nitrates and iron being among the most important. There are large timber tracts in the central and southern zones of Chile with some timber being exported. Oil was found in 1945 in Tierra del Fuego, in the far south, with crude oil being refined in the central part of the country. Pulp, paper, cement and other building materials are also manufactured locally. Other industries are food products, sugar refining and manufacture of textiles.

Energy: Chile produces more coal than any other South American country, although this is not of the best quality. Oil and natural gas are produced and refined in the country and are sufficient for approximately 50 percent of the country's needs. There is some imported crude oil. The production of steel is increasing and there is a steel plant near Concepción.

Agriculture: Central Chile is dominated by large *estancias*. This central zone is an area approximately 30 miles wide that lies between the coastal range and the Andes Mountains. In southern Chile the farms are smaller and the climate is too harsh for most forms of farming. About one-third of Chileans work in agriculture but the methods are not always the most efficient and modern, so Chile cannot supply all its own needs. Major crops are wheat, barley, oats, rye and a variety of fruits for which it is famous. There is a small but expanding wine industry.

Media: There are approximately 40 newspapers printed in Chile with a circulation of 945,000 readers. Only a small percentage of people own a television. Commercial radio is very popular and many people have radio sets. Chile has two television stations.

Glossary

Antarctic Treaty A treaty signed in 1959 by countries interested in exploration and research in Antarctica. The treaty dedicated the continent to peaceful objectives and restricted its use for military purposes.

Aymara Indians South American Indians, originally from Peru and Bolivia.

Caliche The crust on the surface of the Atacama Desert formed by sodium nitrate.

Cellulose A constituent of plants: cellulose in trees is used in the manufacture of paper.

Chono Indians A tribe of Indians who live in the southern regions of Chile.

Cueca The national dance of Chile.

Distill To purify and concentrate alcohol or other liquid by heating it into steam and then collecting the condensed vapor.

Estancia A large estate or cattle ranch.

Guanaco A South American animal which is similar to the llama, and belongs to the same camel family.

Infusion A liquid in which an herb has been soaked.

Molluscs Soft animals without backbones, usually with a hard shell. Mussels, clams, cuttlefish and octopuses are molluscs.

Mummies Human bodies that have been preserved for many centuries.

Nitrate Sodium nitrate, or saltpeter, which occurs in the Atacama Desert.

Oasis A fertile area occurring in a desert.

Osier A flexible willow branch or twig, used for making baskets or furniture.

Pagan Someone who is not a Christian, Moslem or Jew; heathen.

Pisco A drink similar to brandy, distilled from muscat grapes.

Reoxygenation The ability to take in oxygen very fast.

Rodeo A sport involving a high degree of horsemanship.

Silicosis A lung disease, caused by breathing in tiny particles of certain kinds of mineral dust.

Venerate To hold in deep respect.

Vicuña An animal similar to the llama, with fine soft wool.

Zampoña A wind instrument.

Index